GUILD MUSICIANSHIP

Requirements for the Irreducible Minimum Musicianship Test
and All the Musicianship Phases of the National Guild of
Piano Teachers Auditions

Edited by
Eula Ashworth Lindfors

SCALES

CHORDS and CADENCES

ARPEGGIOS

TRANSPOSITION

SIGHT-READING

EAR-TRAINING

Copyright © 1961, 1964, 1974 by Summy-Birchard Music
division of Summy-Birchard Inc.
All rights reserved   Printed in U.S.A.

ISBN: 0-87487-638-9

Summy-Birchard Inc.
exclusively distributed by
Alfred Publishing Co., Inc.

2

Scales

Elementary A

IMMT - None

MP - Majors starting on white keys, one octave hands separately.

A **major scale** is formed according to this pattern of whole and half steps:

1   1   1/2   1   1   1   1/2

Notice that these scales are fingered alike with the exception of the left hand of B and the right hand of F.

• Exercises in this book are notated to avoid leger lines as much as possible, but needn't be played in the octave written.

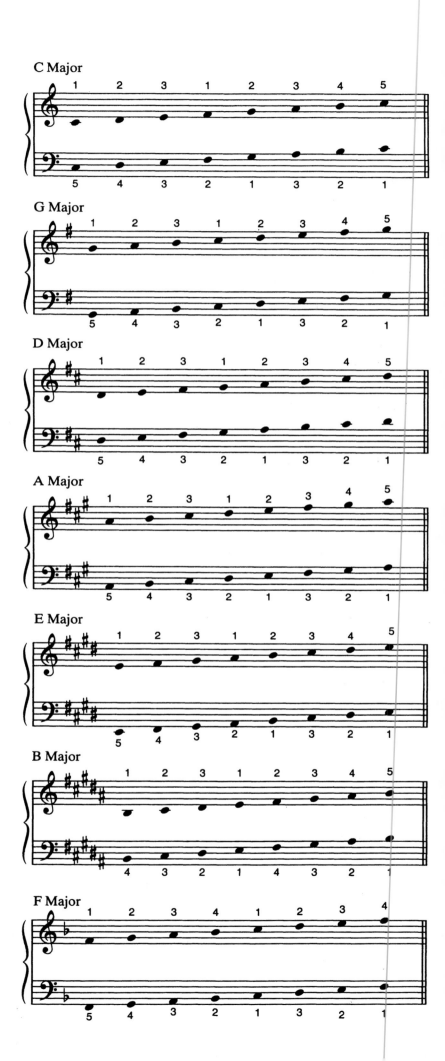

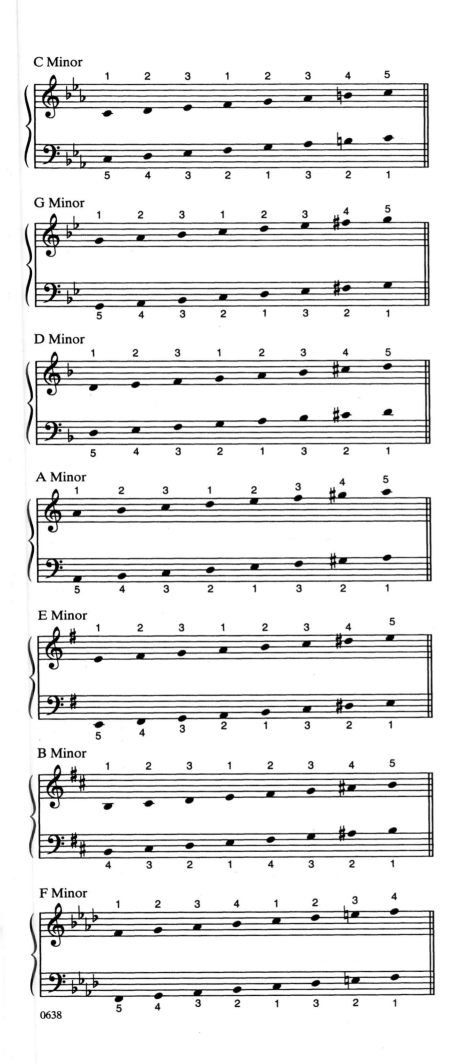

Scales

Elementary B and C
IMMT - Scales divided
between the hands, thus:

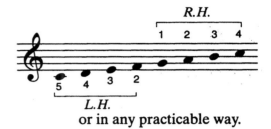

or in any practicable way.

Elementary D
IMMT - Right hand alone, one octave
ascending and descending,
followed by the left hand
doing the same.

Elementary C and D
MP - Harmonic minors
(relative or parallel)
starting on white keys
in addition to majors on page 2,
one octave hands together

The **natural minor** scale is formed
by lowering the 3rd, 6th, and 7th
tones a half step of its parallel
major (on the same tone). The re-
sulting signature is the same as that
of its **relative major** (three half
steps up). In the **harmonic minor**
the 7th tone is raised a half step by
an accidental.

*Notice that the fingering of the minor
scale is the same as that of the major
on the same tone.*

Scales   Intermediate A and B

MP - Majors and harmonic minors (relative or parallel)
in addition to scales on pages 2 and 3, one octave
hands together.

*Notice that in these scales the 4th finger of the right hand plays
Bb (A#) and the 4th finger of the left plays the 4th note, except
in those with 6 and 7 sharps or flats, where it plays Gb (F#).*

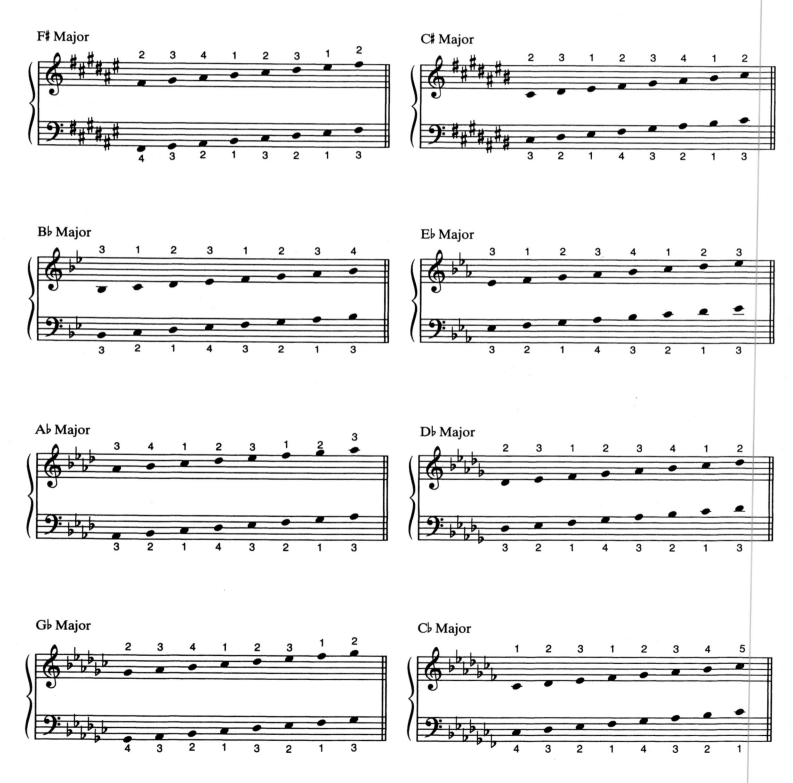

Intermediate A and B continued   **Scales**

Enharmonic scales are written differently but sound the same.

Notice that the fingering of these minor scales is the same as that of the major starting on the same tone, except:

B♭ (A♯) Minor ⎫ L.H. 4th finger   F♯ Minor ⎫ R.H. 4th finger
E♭ (D♯) Minor ⎰ on G♭ (F♯)   C♯ Minor ⎰ on 2nd note

F♯ Minor

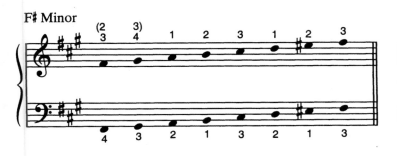

C♯ Minor

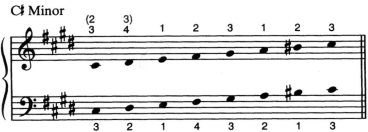

B♭ Minor enharmonic with -

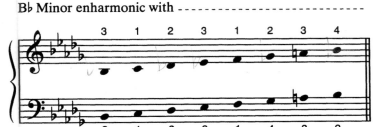

A♯ Minor

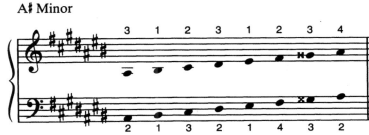

E♭ Minor enharmonic with -

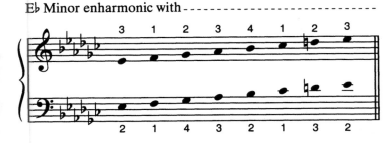

D♯ Minor

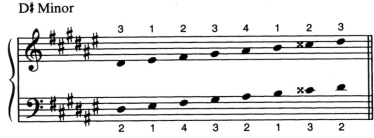

A♭ Minor enharmonic with - G♯ Minor

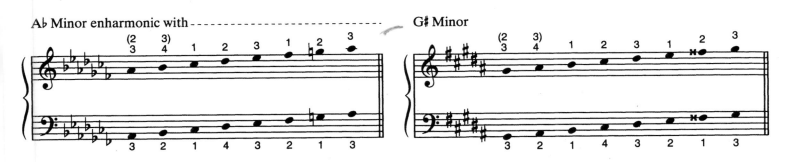

Scales

Intermediate A, B, C, D, E, F
IMMT - Two octaves hands together.

Intermediate C, D, E, F
MP - All major harmonic minors (relative or parallel), two octaves hands together.

Notice that two-octave scales are fingered the same as one-octave, except that the thumb is used in place of the 5th finger where it is necesary to continue.

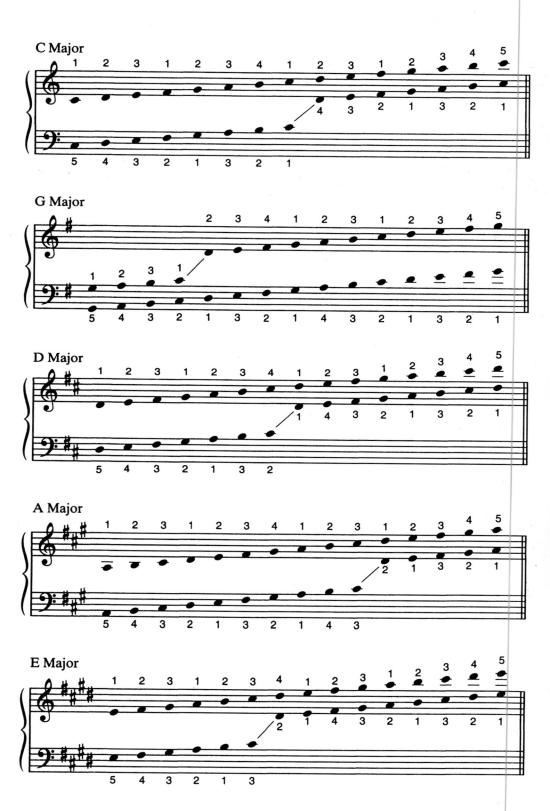

Scales
Intermediate C, D, E, F continued

Scales
Intermediate C, D, E, F continued

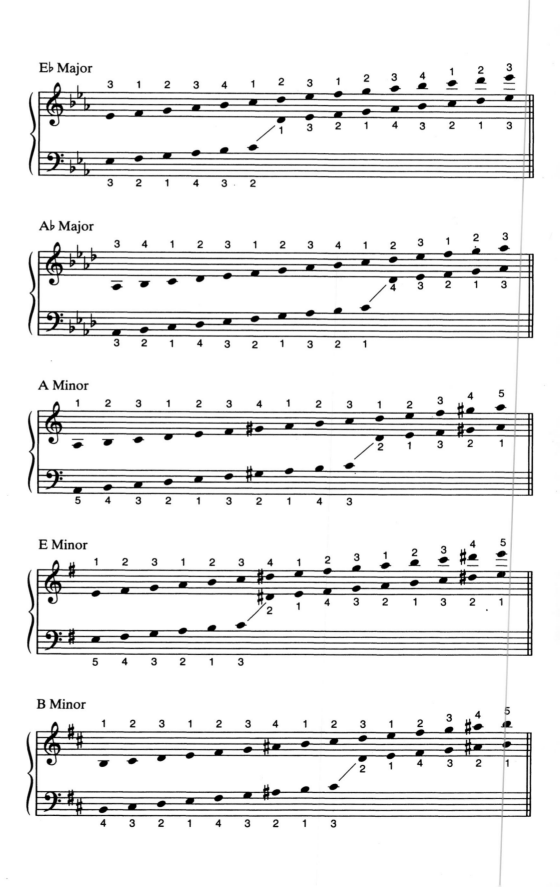

Scales
Intermediate C, D, E, F continued

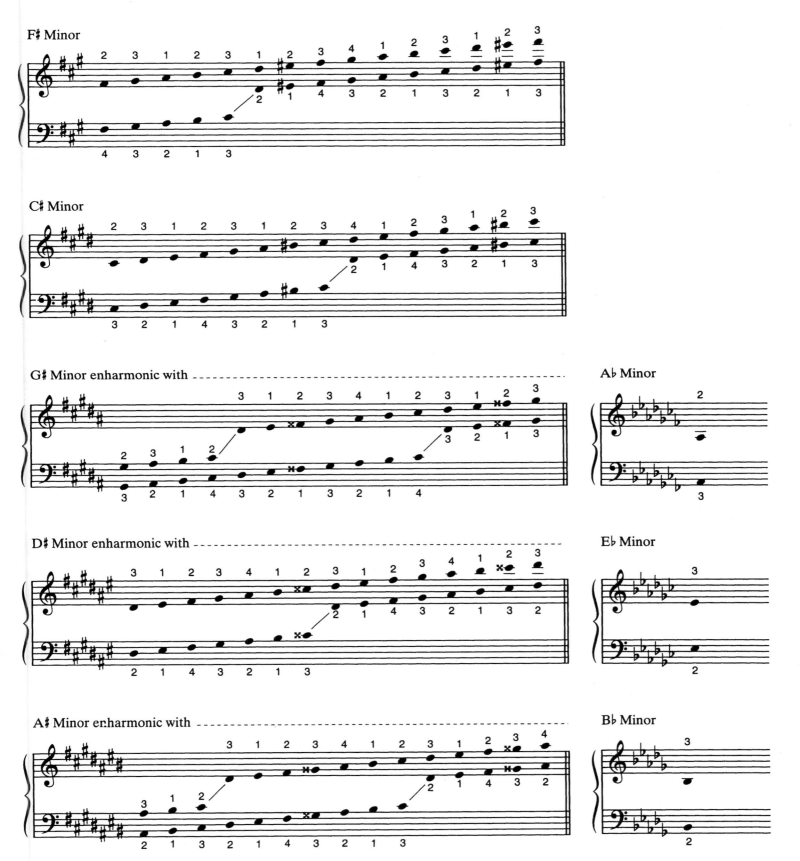

Scales
Intermediate C, D, E, F continued

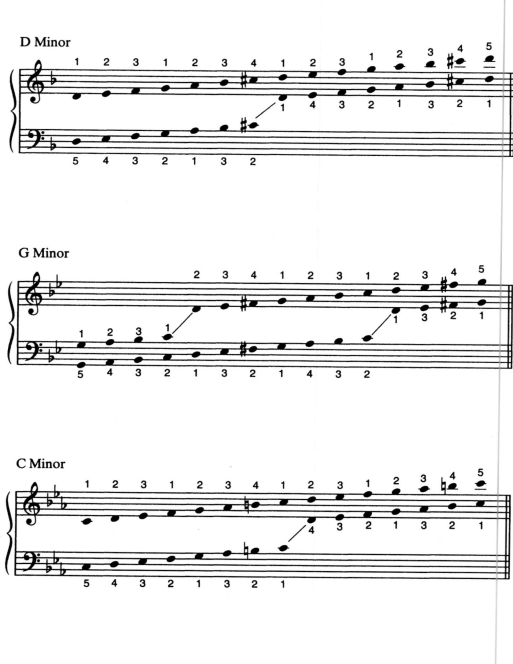

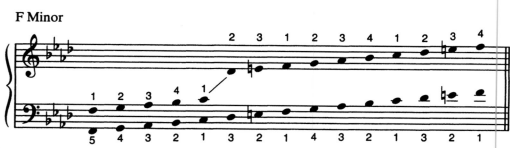

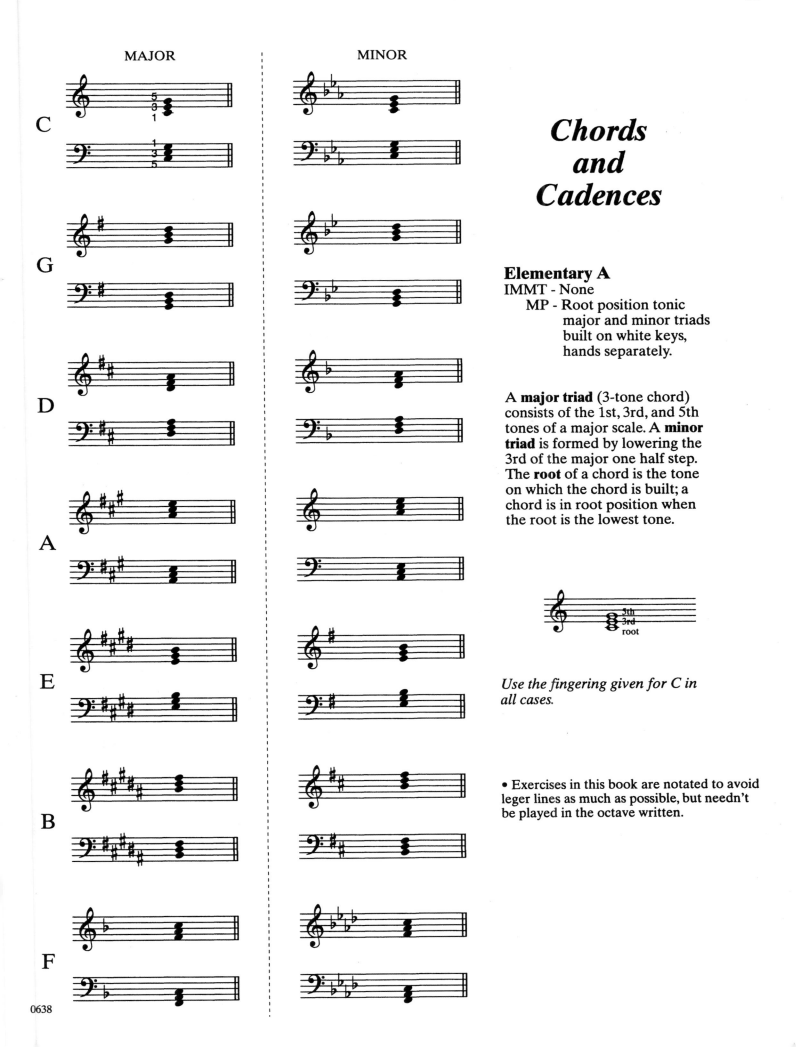

MAJOR MINOR

C
G
D
A
E
B
F

Chords and Cadences

Elementary A
IMMT - None
   MP - Root position tonic
     major and minor triads
     built on white keys,
     hands separately.

A **major triad** (3-tone chord) consists of the 1st, 3rd, and 5th tones of a major scale. A **minor triad** is formed by lowering the 3rd of the major one half step. The **root** of a chord is the tone on which the chord is built; a chord is in root position when the root is the lowest tone.

Use the fingering given for C in all cases.

• Exercises in this book are notated to avoid leger lines as much as possible, but needn't be played in the octave written.

0638

Chords and Cadences

Elementary B and C
IMMT - Cadence, hands separately, following this pattern of progression: tonic chord root position, to the nearest position of the **dominant** chord, and back to the tonic.

The **tonic** chord is built on I of the scale, the **dominant**, on V.

The dominant-tonic closing progression is called an **authentic cadence.**

Use the fingering given for C in all cases.

Chords and *Cadences

Elementary C and D

MP - Three positions of tonic major and minor triads on white-key roots, hands together.

A triad can be in three different positions: with the root, with the 3rd, or with the 5th as the lowest tone. When any tone but the root is the lowest, the chord is called **an inversion.**

Use the fingering given for C in all cases.

*MP - Same as IMMT Elementary D (see page 14), except hands together.

CHORDS and CADENCES

Elementary D

IMMT - I V I cadence from each position of the tonic triad, hands separately.

F♯ Major

F♯ Minor

C♯ Major

C♯ Minor

F Major

F Minor

B♭ Major

B♭ Minor

E♭ Major

E♭ Minor

A♭ Major

A♭ Minor

16

*Chords and Cadences

Intermediate A, B

MP - I IV I V I cadence
from root position
of tonic triad;
chords in both hands.

Intermediate C, D, E, F

MP - I IV I V I cadence
from each position
of tonic triad;
chords in both hands.

*MP - See page 20.

Intermediate A, B, C, D, E, F

IMMT - I IV I V I cadence
from each position
of the tonic triad;
hands separately
or together.

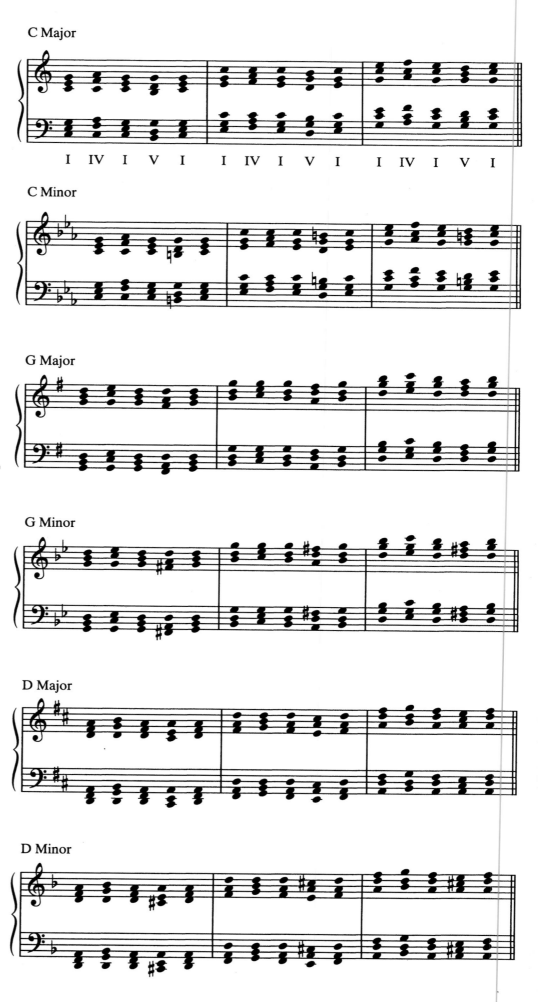

A Major

A Minor

E Major

E Minor

B Major

B Minor

*Chords
and
Cadences*

**Intermediate
A, B, C, D, E, F**
continued

Chords and Cadences

Intermediate A, B, C, D, E, F continued

F♯ Major

F♯ Minor

C♯ Major

C♯ Minor

F Major

F Minor

Bb Major

Bb Minor

Eb Major

Eb Minor

Ab Major

Ab Minor

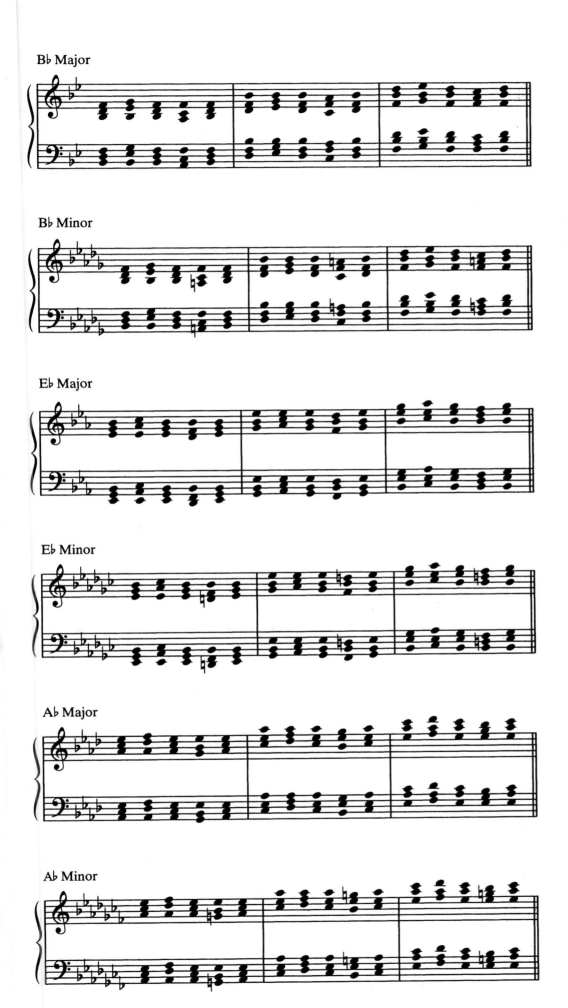

Chords
and
Cadences

Intermediate
A, B, C, D, E, F
continued

Chords and Cadences

Intermediate A and B

MP - Three positions of
tonic major and minor
triads, in addition to
those on page 13.

Intermediate C, D, E, F

MP - Three positions of diminished
and augmented triads,
in addition to triads on page 13.

A **diminished** triad
is formed by lowering the 5th of a minor triad.

Bb   MAJOR/MINOR

Eb

Ab

F#

C#

An **augmented** triad
is formed by raising the 5th of a major triad.

Arpeggios

IMMT - None

Elementary A and B
MP - None.

Elementary C and D
MP - Root position only, tonic major and minor triads starting on white keys, two octaves hands separately or together.

Intermediate A and B
MP - Root position only, all tonic major and minor triads, two octaves hands together.

Intermediate C, D, E, F
MP - Three positions, all tonic major and minor triads, two octaves hands together.

To facilitate learning, arpeggios are grouped according to fingering rather than given in order of the circle of 5ths.

•Exercises in this book are notated to avoid leger lines as much as possible, but needn't be played in the octave written.

all white keys *(all fingered alike)*

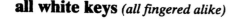

C Major

D Minor

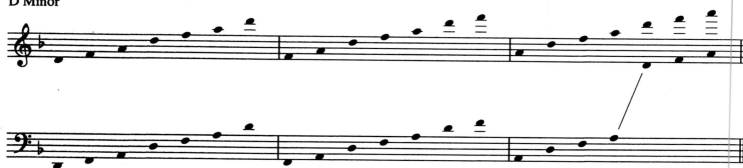

Notice that the right thumb and left fifth finger play the first notes of all chord positions starting on white keys. In positions starting on black keys, the right thumb plays the lowest white key and the left thumb, the highest. All-black-key chords are fingered like those with all white keys.

Arpeggios
Intermediate C, D, E, F continued

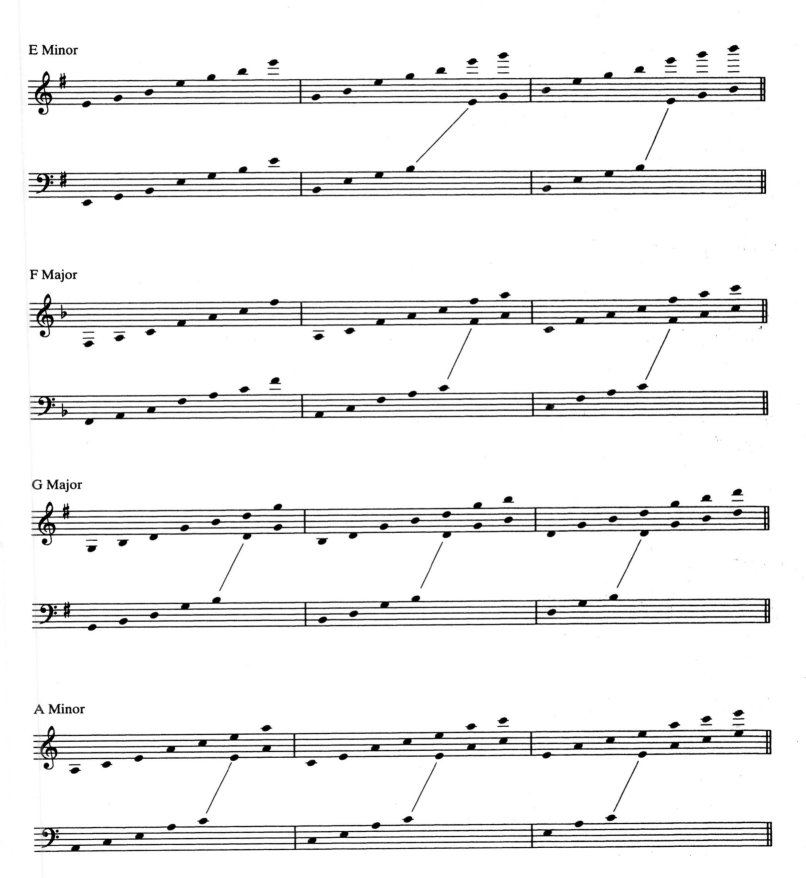

Arpeggios
Intermediate C, D, E, F continued

one black key

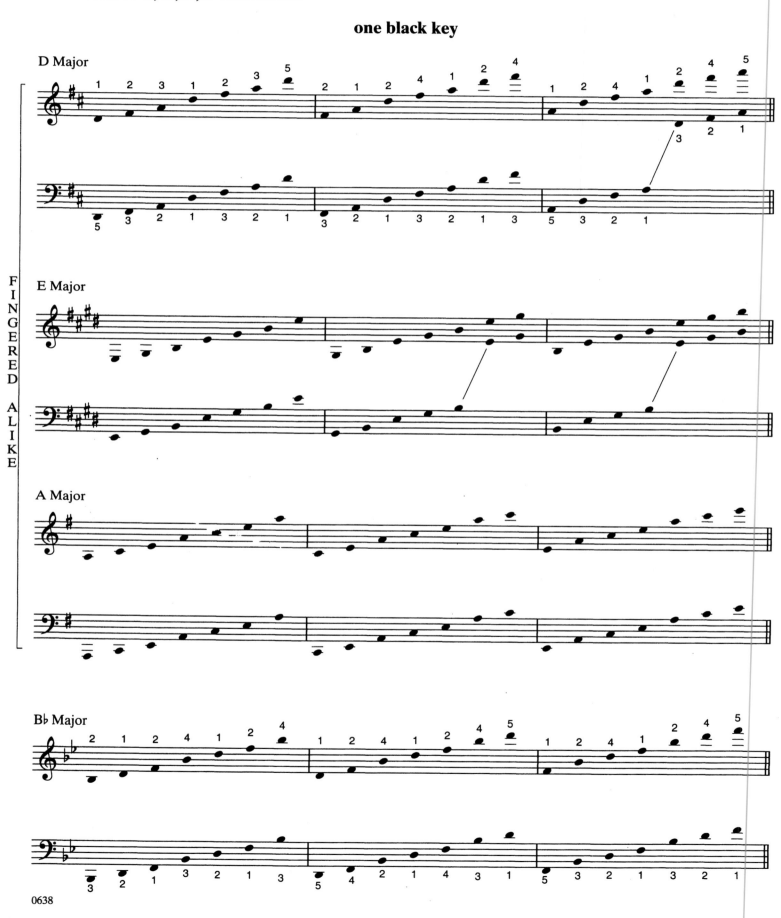

Arpeggios
Intermediate C, D, E, F continued

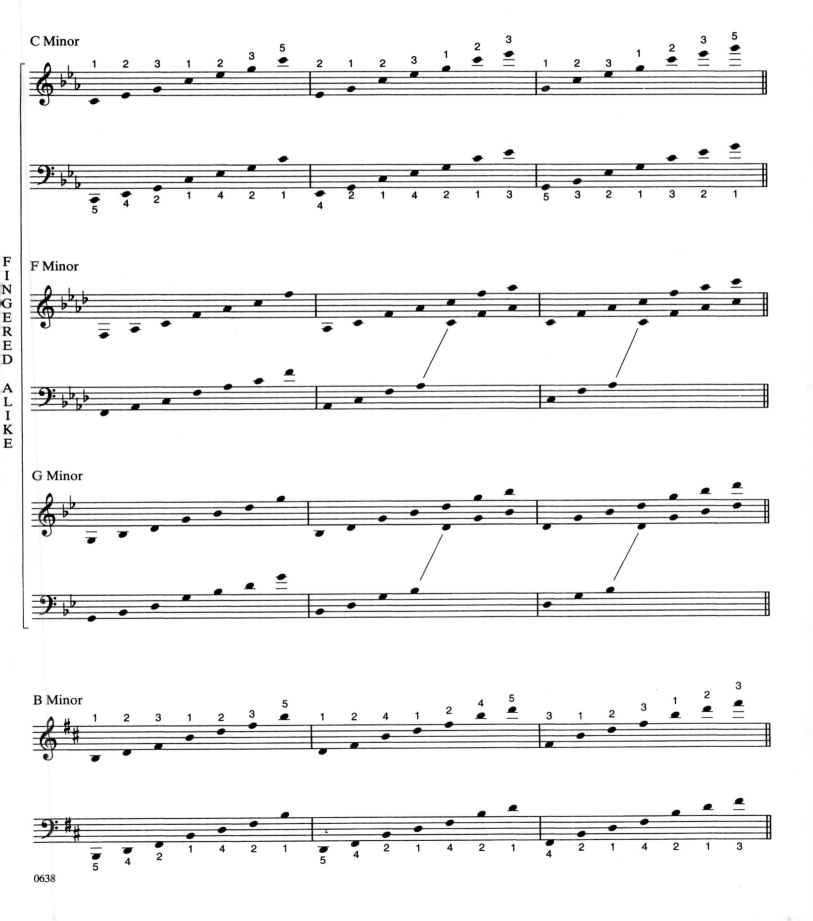

26

Arpeggios Intermediate C, D, E, F   two black keys

FINGERED ALIKE

C♯ Major

C♯ Minor

E♭ Major

F♯ Minor

G♯ Minor

0638

Intermediate C, D, E, F continued Arpeggios

Scales

Preparatory A, B, C, D
IMMT - Four octaves hands together, parallel motion.

Preparatory A and B
MP - All majors and harmonic minors four octaves, parallel motion.

♩ = 72, minimum tempo

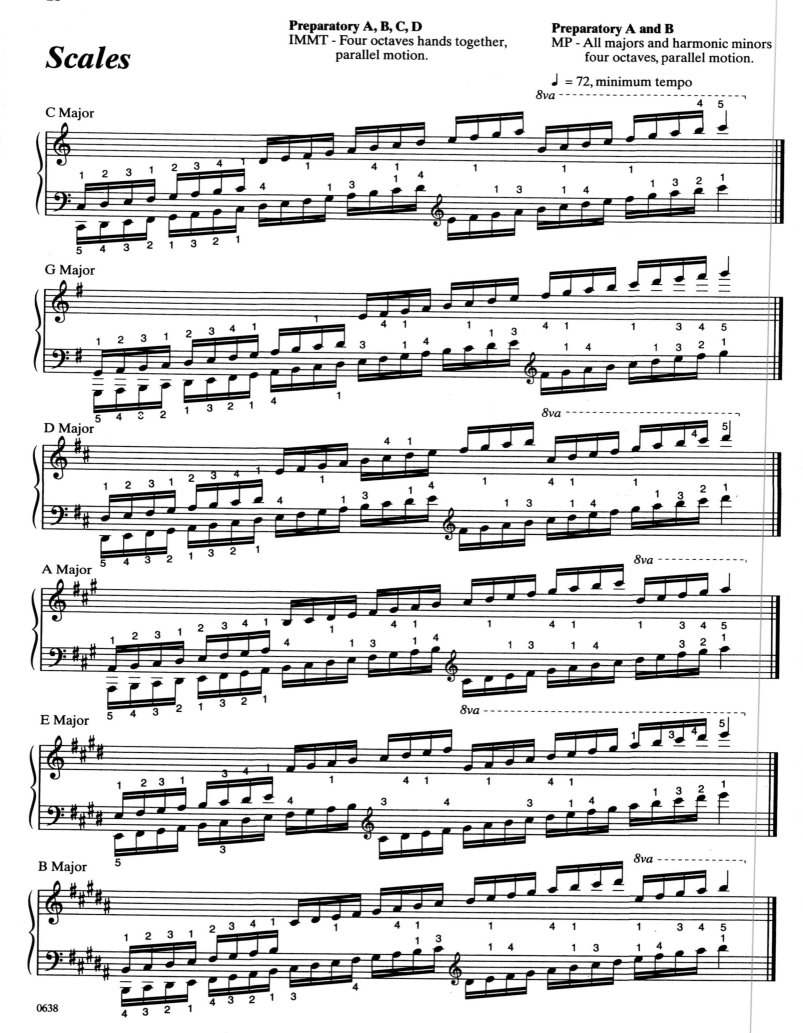

Scales

Preparatory A and B continued

SCALES
Preparatory A and B continued

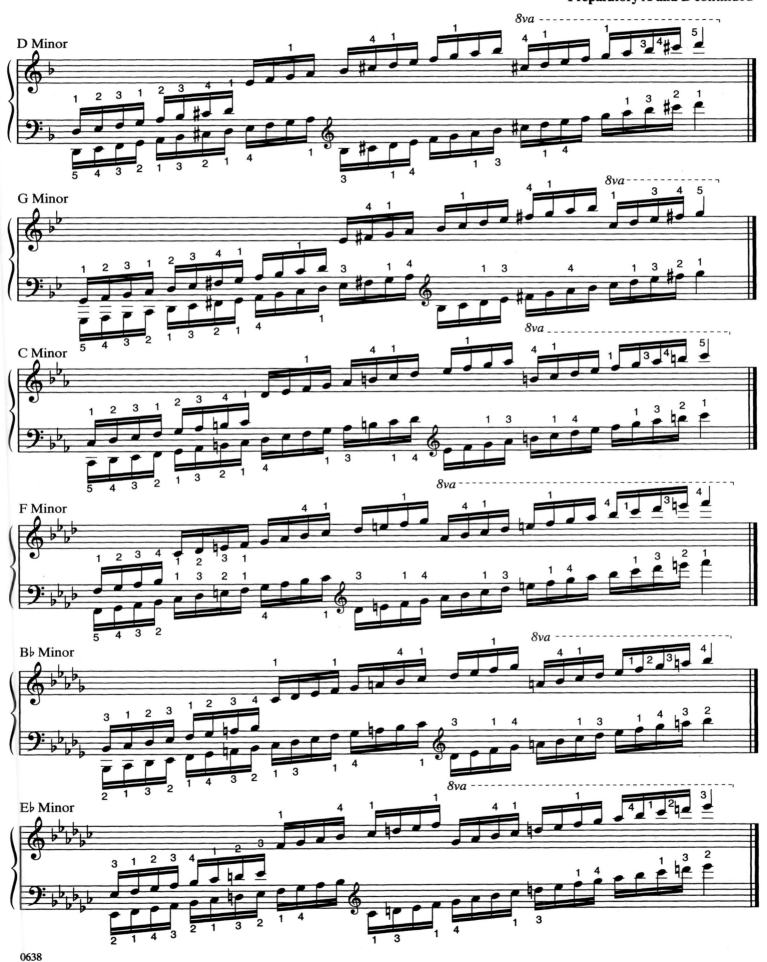

SCALES
Preparatory C and D

MP - All majors and minors
two octaves, contrary motion
in addition to scales on pp. 28-31.
♩ = 88, minimum tempo

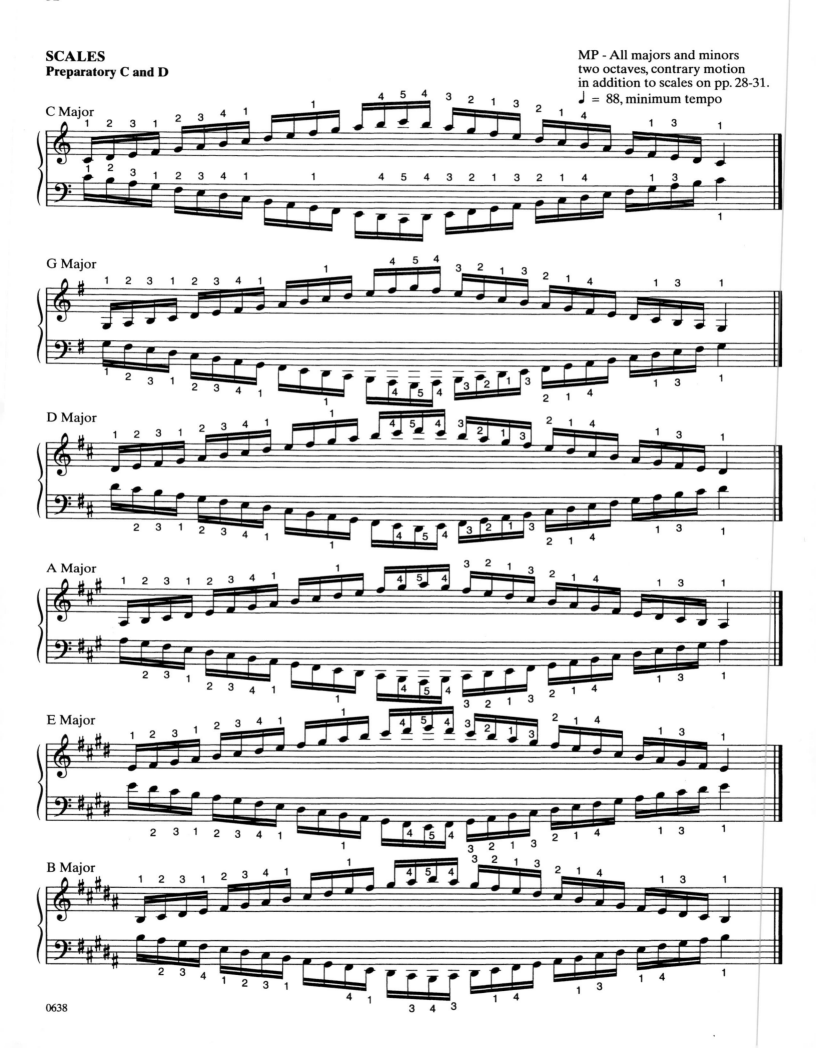

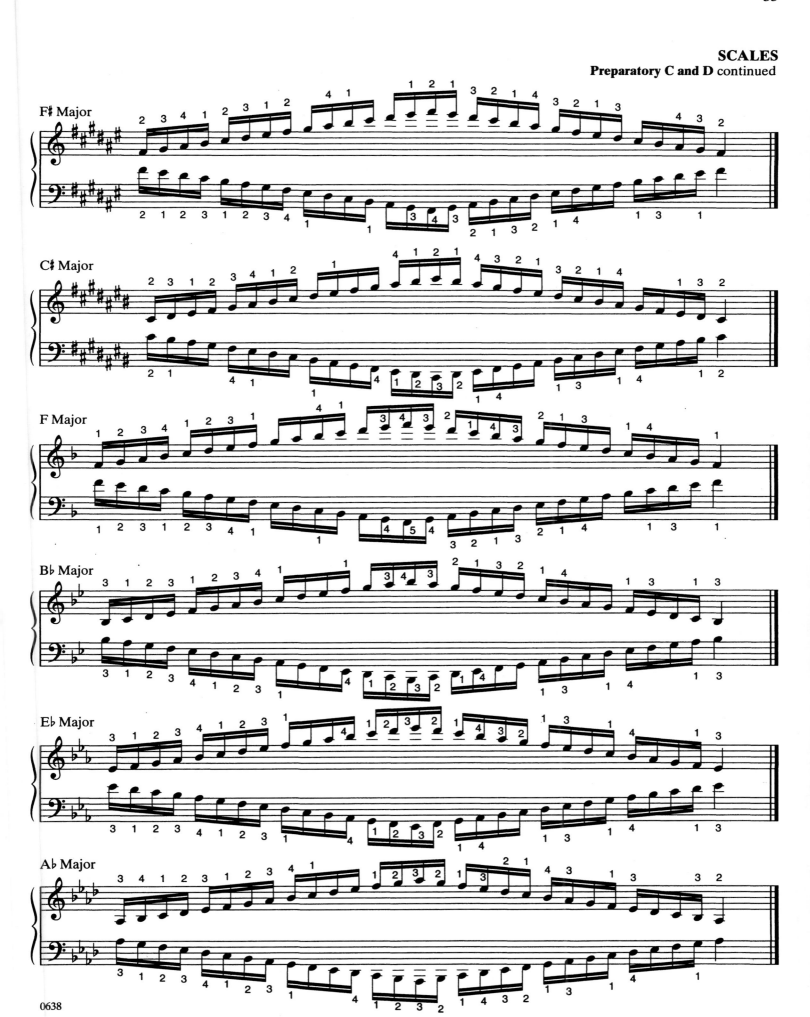

SCALES
Preparatory C and D continued

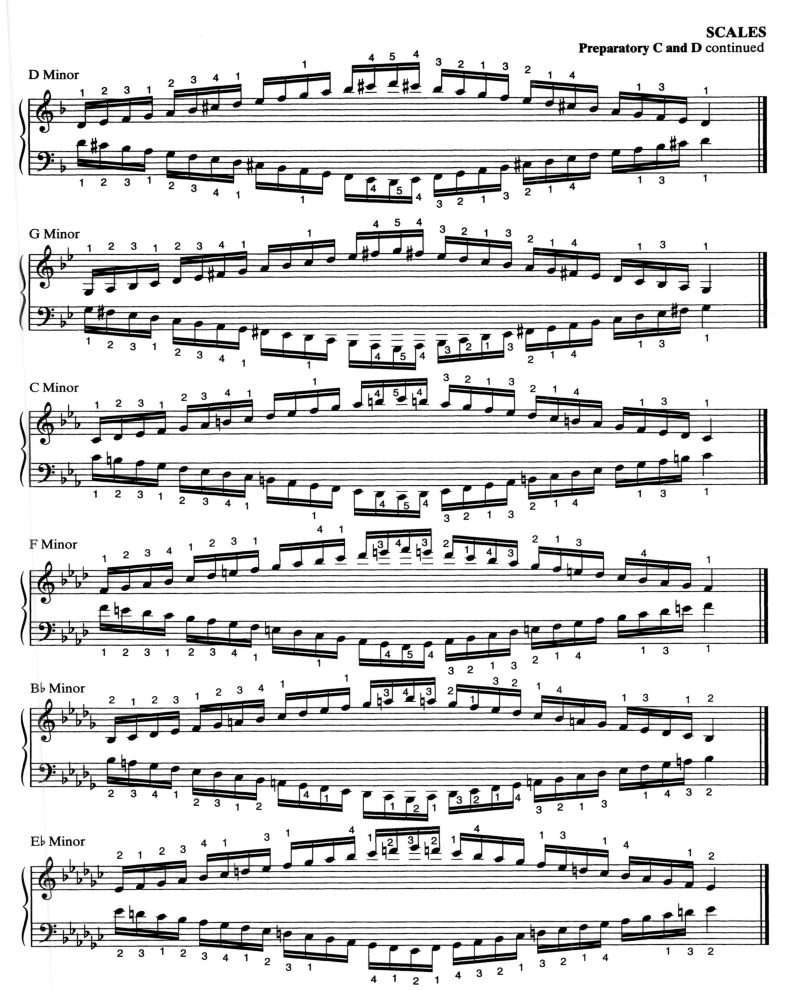

Chords and Cadences

Preparatory A, B, C, D
IMMT - Chords in the following pattern of progression:
root position and inversions of I IV V V7 I
hands together.

Chords and Cadences

IMMT - **Preparatory A, B, C, D**
continued

C Minor

G Minor

D Minor

A Minor

E Minor

B Minor

0638

Chords and Cadences

IMMT - **Preparatory A, B, C, D**
continued

F♯ Major

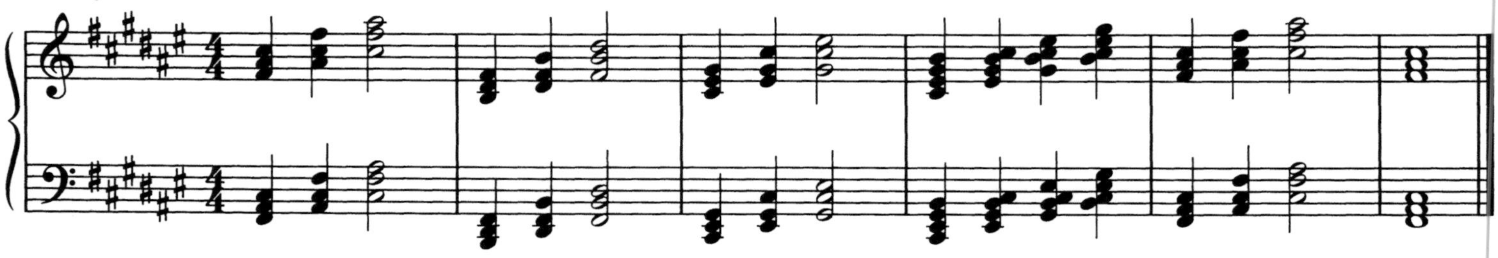

C♯ Major

F Major

B♭ Major

E♭ Major

A♭ Major

Chords and Cadences
IMMT - **Preparatory A, B, C, D**
continued

Chords
and
Cadences

Preparatory A and B
MP - I IV I V V7 I
    cadence in all keys.

MP - *Dominant 7th
    chords in root
    position.

The **dominant 7th** chord
is so called because it is
built on the dominant (V)
of the scale, and the inter-
val from its root to highest
tone is a 7th. The tones of
V7 are the same in both
major and minor keys
having the same tonic.

MP - *Diminished 7th
    chords in root
    position.

The **diminished 7th**
chord consists of a
diminished triad with
diminished 7th (three
minor 3rds of three
half steps each).

*First chord each
example on page 46.

A Major

A Minor

E Major

E Minor

B Major

B Minor

Chords and Cadences
Preparatory A and B continued

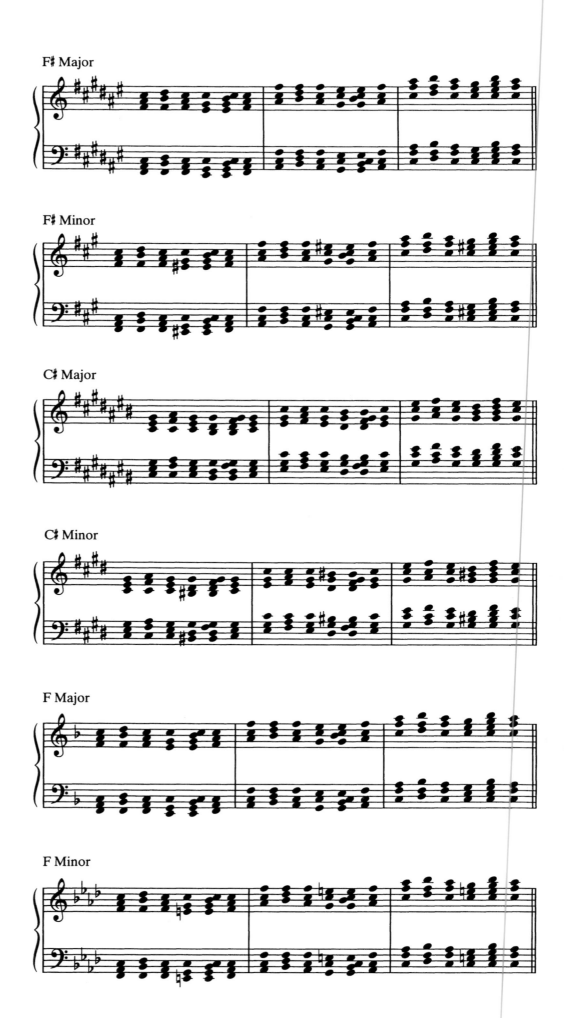

F# Major

F# Minor

C# Major

C# Minor

F Major

F Minor

B♭ Major

B♭ Minor

E♭ Major

E♭ Minor

A♭ Major

A♭ Minor

44

Chords and Cadences

Preparatory C and D
MP - Plagal cadence in all keys, in addition to previous
   requirements.
A **plagal cadence** is a subdominant-tonic closing progression.
MP - Dominant and diminished seventh chords in all positions (see p. 46).

plagal cadence

C Major   C Minor

I IV I   I IV I   I IV I   I IV I   I IV I   I IV I

G Major   G Minor

D Major   D Minor

A Major   A Minor

E Major   E Minor

B Major   B Minor

Chords and Cadences
Preparatory C and D continued

plagal cadence

Chords and Cadences

Preparatory C and D continued

Arpeggios

Preparatory A and B
MP - Major and minor triads in all positions, three octaves each.
Diminished 7ths, root position,
three octaves (see p. 50).
♩ = 72, minimum tempo

all white keys

To facilitate learning, arpeggios are grouped according to fingering rather than given in order of the circle of 5ths.

0638

Arpeggios

Preparatory A and B continued

one black key

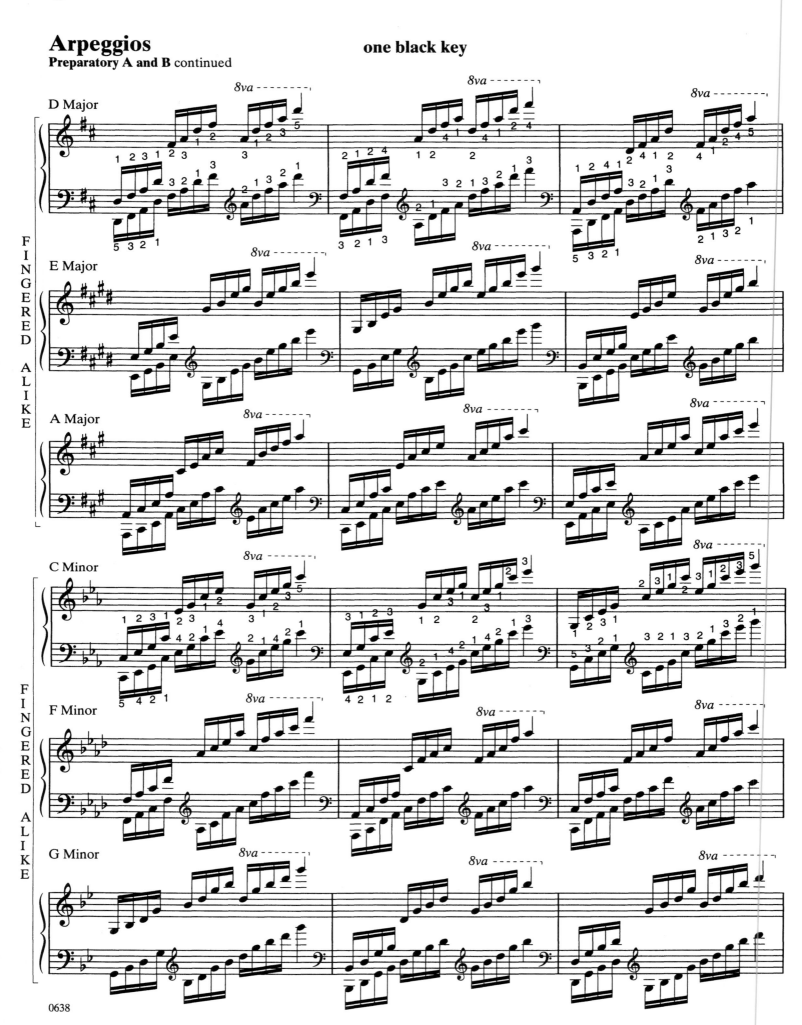

Arpeggios
Preparatory A and B continued

two black keys

F
I
N
G
E
R
E
D

A
L
I
K
E

Arpeggios
Preparatory A and B continued

one black key

Diminished Seventh - *All seventh-chord arpeggios starting on white keys are played with successive fingers from the thumb in the right hand and the fifth finger in the left. In positions starting on black keys, the right thumb plays the lowest white key and the left thumb, the highest.*

Arpeggios
Preparatory A and B continued

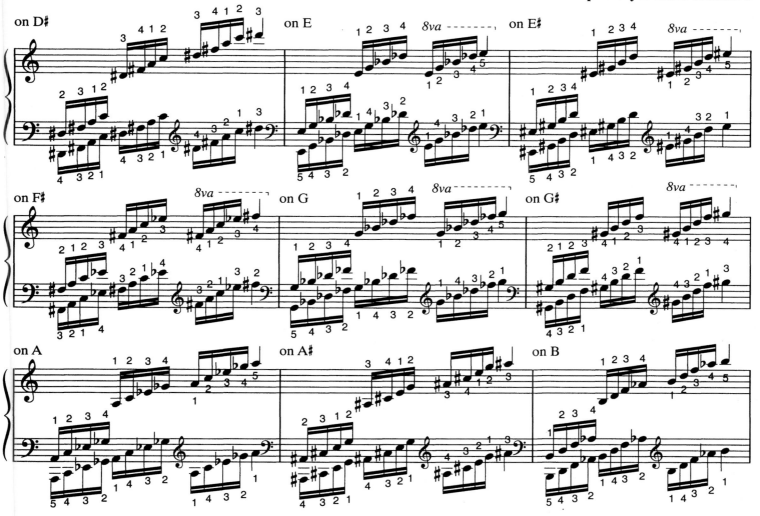

MP - major and minor triads in all positions, four octaves each
(continue arpeggios pp. 47-50 for another octave).
- Dominant 7ths, all positions, four octaves
- Diminished 7ths, all positions, four octaves

Preparatory C and D

Dominant Seventh - *Continue all arpeggios for four octaves,
ending on the highest note with the finger indicated after the dash.*

Arpeggios
Preparatory C and D continued

of D Major and Minor

of A Major and Minor

of E Major and Minor

of B Major and Minor

of F♯ Major and Minor

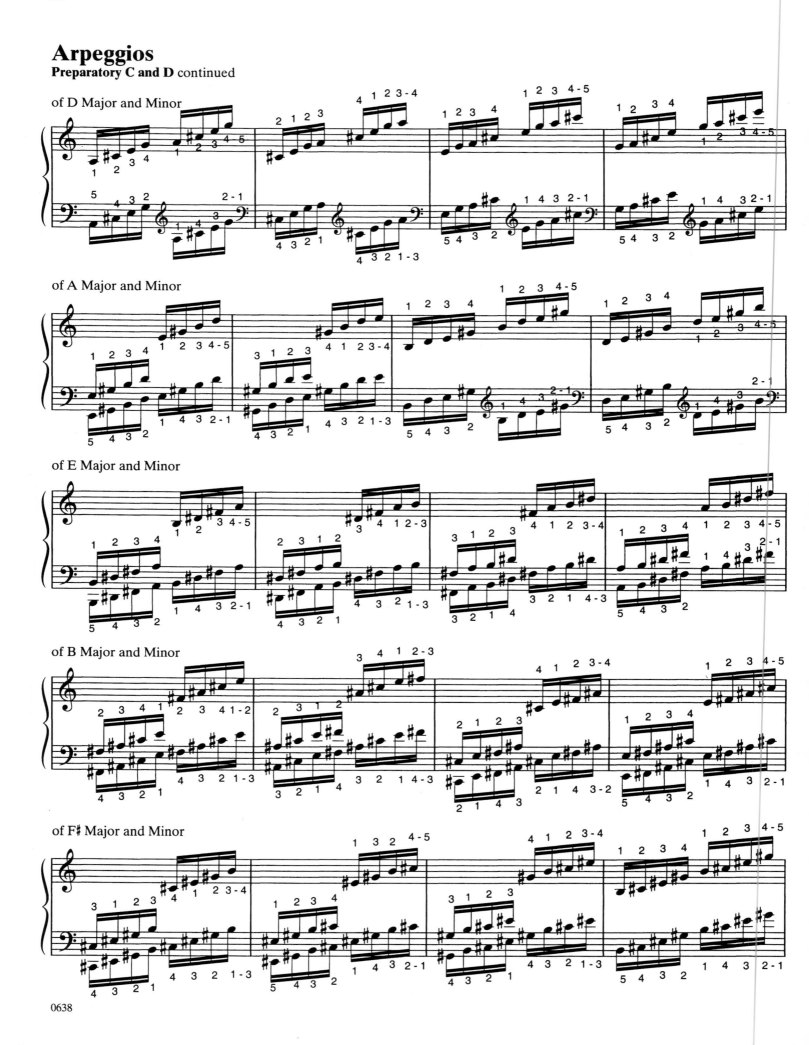

of C♯ Major and Minor

of F Major and Minor

of B♭ Major and Minor

of E♭ Major and Minor

of A♭ Major and Minor

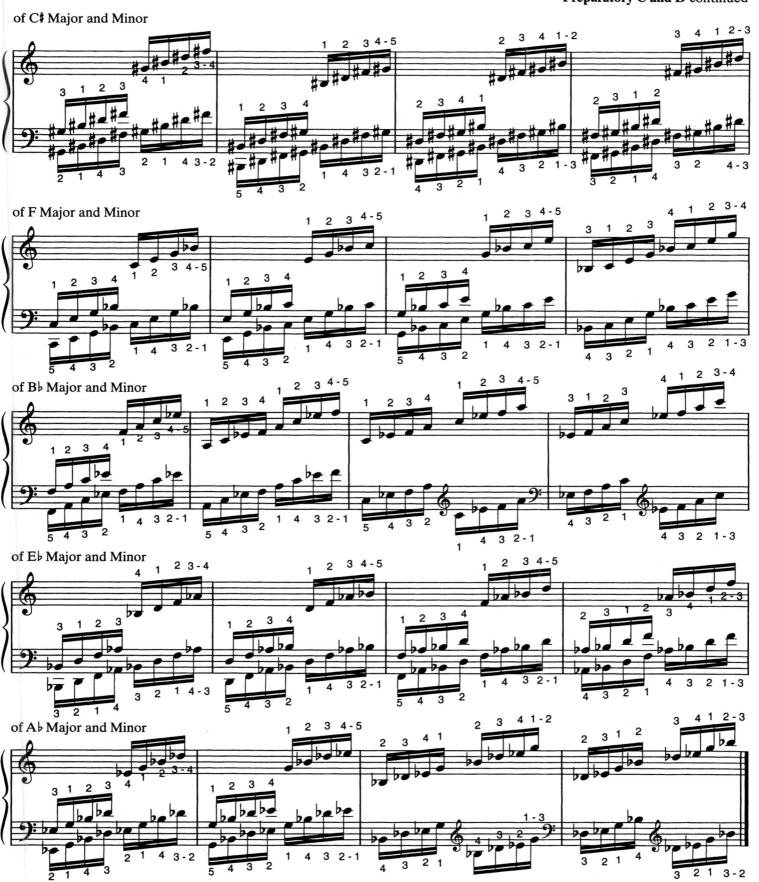

Diminished Seventh - *Since all the intervals within a diminished seventh chord are equal (all minor 3rds), inversions and root positions on the same tone are identical. Therefore, for diminished 7th inversions refer to the root position on the desired tone (pp. 50 and 51).*

Transposition

IMMT - None.
Elementary A, B, C, D
Intermediate A, B
MP - None.
Intermediate C, D, E, F
MP - A Grade 2 piece of pupil's choice.
Preparatory A and B
MP - A Grade 2 piece of pupil's choice.
Preparatory C and D
MP - A Grade 3 piece into three keys of pupil's choice.

Transposing a musical composition means playing (or writing) it in a key different from that in which it is written. Therefore, each tone will be a certain distance higher or lower than its original pitch. The easiest transposition is a half step higher or lower. The ability to transpose requires knowledge of key signatures, chords, and intervals – both from one tone to the next (horizontally), as well as those forming chords (vertically).

Brass Buttons

WILLIAM SCHER

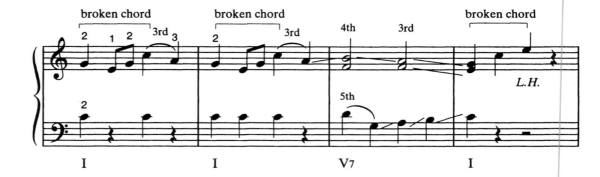

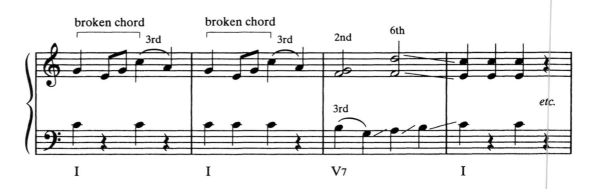

© 1956 by SUMMY-BIRCHARD COMPANY
All Rights Reserved

As an example, the first part of *Brass Buttons* by William Scher is given in its original key of C, also transposed a 4th down to G. Movement by step within the scale is indicated by lines between notes, and other intervals and harmonies to notice especially are marked. It is usually advisable to keep the original fingering in transposing.

Brass Buttons

WILLIAM SCHER

Key of G

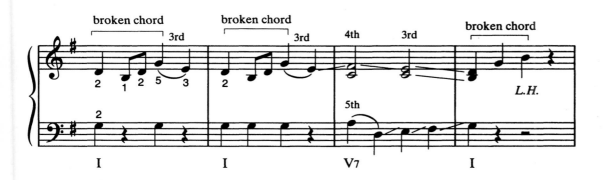

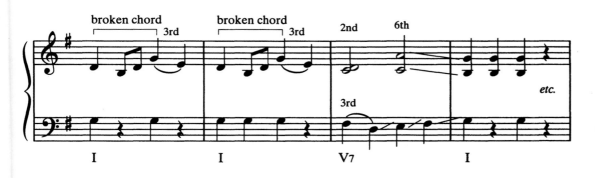

© 1956 by SUMMY-BIRCHARD COMPANY
All Rights Reserved

Sight-Reading

IMMT - None.
Elementary A, B, C, D
Intermediate A, B
MP - None.
Intermediate C, D, E, F
MP - Two Grade 2 pieces of audition judge's selection.
Preparatory A and B
MP - Two Grade 2 pieces of audition judge's selection.
Preparatory C and D
MP - Two grade 3 pieces of audition judge's selection.

The ability to sight-read piano music depends mainly on keeping the eyes on the music and not looking down at the keyboard; on reading by groups of notes rather than one note at a time; and on looking ahead to see what is coming. Above all, it requires to keep going rhythmically even though there are mistakes.

Before starting to play, the clefs and key and time signatures should be noticed. The title and tempo mark should be looked to for clues to the idea of the piece. (It may be necessary to play slower than the indicated tempo, however, in order to keep a steady pace.)

The arrows in the following piece of music show the only places where it may be necessary to look at the keys.

11-10-14
Excellent!

Four O'Clock

A. LOUIS SCARMOLIN

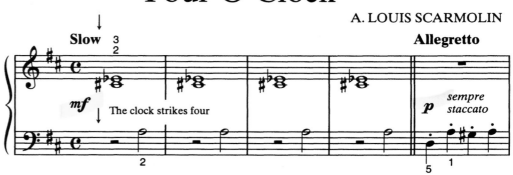

© 1957 by SUMMY-BIRCHARD COMPANY
All Rights Reserved

The Circle of Fifths

The 12 keys can be arranged in order of 5ths on a circle—sharp keys to the right, flat keys to the left—with enharmonic sharp an[d] flat scales coinciding at the bottom of the circle.

Major scales are indicated by capitals and minors by small letters. Closely related keys (those with a difference of one sharp o[r] one flat) appear next to each other in the circle.

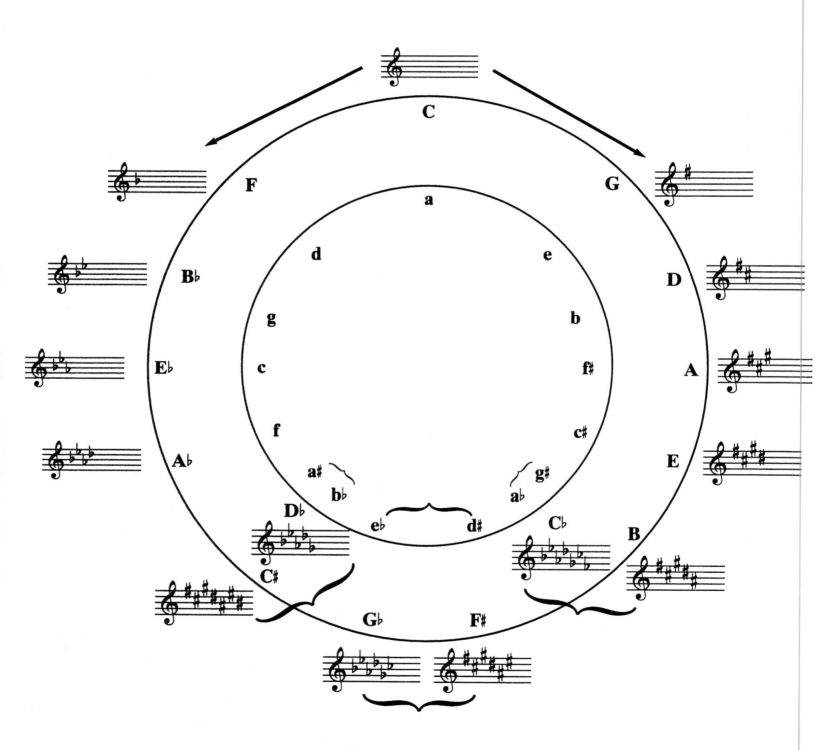

Ear-Training

IMMT—None

Elementary A and B

MP—Listen to triads and tell whether they are major or minor.

Elementary C and D
Intermediate A and B

MP—Listen to scales, triads, and intervals
and tell whether they are major or minor.

Intermediate C, D, E, F

MP—In addition to the above,
listen to augmented
and diminished triads
and distinguish between them.

Preparatory A and B

MP—Be able to recognize
all intervals, scales, and chords

—Listen for accents
and distinguish between 2/4 and 3/4 measure.

Preparatory C and D

MP—In addition to the above,
feel the pulsation
in 2/4 and 3/4 measure
and identify note values.